Being an Empath Kid

Christie Lyons AND Jessie Welsh

Printed in China
First Printing, 2016
ISBN: 978-0-9925202-1-2

White Light Publishing House

www.whitelightpublishingau.com

A super big thank you to Sienna, who chose the new cover design. Never underestimate how amazing you really are. xoxo

Empathy is when we understand and share other people's feelings. It's what makes other people matter to us.

We are all born with empathy.
We learn all about it when we are babies, and
sometimes even before we are born.

Empathy is how we know when someone might need a hug because they are feeling sad, or how you know to react to someone if they're in a grumpy mood.

Some people though, are born with much more than just empathy. Some of us share other people's feelings, thoughts and energy much, much more.

This is what is known as being an **Empath**.
Being an Empath is a wonderful gift, but can also be
difficult at times.

Some of the things that you might experience as an Empath could be:

- Liking to spend a lot of time alone
- Enjoying spending time with animals
- Getting upset, angry, or grumpy a lot
- Feeling tired a lot of the time
- Having a wonderful imagination and enjoying creative activities
- Not liking loud noises or crowds
- Being a good listener
- Having psychic abilities

The main gift you have as an Empath is that you know how others feel without them having to tell you. This is because you feel their emotions and energy as well as your own.

This can happen a lot of the time without you even knowing. If you're in a shopping centre or at school, for example, you will pick up on the energies of all the many people around you.

Imagine that you are a magnet, and all of the energy of other people and situations is magnetic too. All of the energy around is drawn to you like this magnet.

It can be difficult sometimes because it's hard to tell the difference between other people's energy and your own.

Feeling other people's energy all the time can tire you out, and can even make you feel sick or in pain.

It is important that you know how to protect yourself from this energy so that you stay healthy and happy.

There are lots of ways that you can do this.

Grounding

You can easily 'ground' yourself by spending time in nature. Take your shoes off and walk around on the grass or dirt with bare feet. When you aren't able to get outside, you can imagine that your feet have roots coming out of the bottom of them and are sinking deep, deep into the earth.

Meditating  Breathing

When you breathe deeply it helps to calm your body and mind. Close your eyes and take ten deep breaths in and out. While you do this, imagine that you are breathing in green healing energy, and breathing out any negative energy or feelings.

White Light Bubble

Another way you can protect yourself is to imagine a bubble full of protective white light that goes all around you. You can use this bubble whenever you feel like you need protection, and only love and positivity will be able to enter through it.

Get Creative!

Using your creative skills is a great way to feel better after being around negative energy. When you are creative, you are using the right side of your brain, and this means that you will also be using your intuition, and doing something that makes you happy.

Clear your energy

Emotions are like waves of energy that get stuck and so it's important that you clear this negative energy regularly. You can ask an adult to use White Sage to clear your energy and your room, or you could use crystals such as Rose Quartz or Black Tourmaline. Another way to clear negative energy is to use sound, such as bells or drums.

Drink lots of water

Not only is water very healthy for you, but it is also helpful in keeping you grounded. As you drink your water, imagine that it is clearing out all negative energy as it flows through your body.

The very best thing that you can do as an Empath is to know the **difference** between your own feelings, and the feelings of other people.

Always remember that while you have the ability to understand other people's emotions, they are not YOURS.

Ask yourself:

"How am I feeling right now?"
"Are these my feelings?"

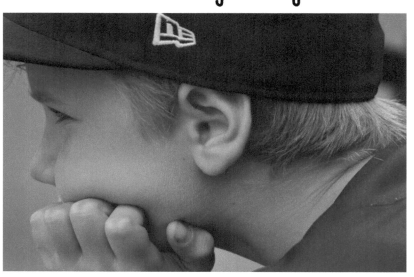

This will help you to know the difference between the feelings that are yours, and the feelings that you have picked up from someone else.

Being an Empath is a wonderful gift and knowing how to manage your gift while you are young will help you for the rest of your life.

Not only will you be able to look after yourself, but you can help many other people too.

Parent's Information

Having a child with the gift of being an Empath is a beautiful experience, however it can also be quite challenging. We created this book to assist children to understand their gift at a young age, so that they may have the tools to manage their gift in a healthy and loving way, both in their childhood as well as through their adult life.

It is important that parents and caregivers are supportive of this gift and take the time to understand the possible related behaviours that a child may express while they try to understand what it means to be an Empath.

If you would like more information on ways to support your child, please feel free to contact Christie at White Light for the Soul.

Email: whitelightforthesoul@outlook.com

CPSIA information can be obtained
at www.ICGtesting.com
Printed in the USA
BVHW090823270321
603524BV00018B/319